FOR
YOU

A Little Book of Love Poems and Letters

# A Little Book of

# Love

# Poems and Letters

Edited by
Lena Tabori & Natasha Tabori Fried

A Welcome Book

**Andrews McMeel
Publishing**

Kansas City

Designed by Gregory Wakabayashi

*A Little Book of Love Poems and Letters*
compilation copyright © 2001 by Lena Tabori and Natasha Tabori Fried.
All rights reserved. Printed in Singapore. No part of this book may be
used or reproduced in any manner whatsoever without written permission
except in the case of reprints in the context of reviews.
For information, write Andrews McMeel Publishing,
an Andrews McMeel Universal company,
4520 Main Street, Kansas City, Missouri 64111.

ISBN: 0-7407-1470-8

Library of Congress Cataloging-in-Publication Data
00-106962

# Contents

# Let Me Not to the Marriage of True Minds

### William Shakespeare

Let me not to the marriage of true minds
Admit impediments; love is not love
Which alters when it alteration finds,
Or bends with the remover to remove.
O, no, it is an ever-fixed mark
That looks on tempests and is never shaken;
It is the star to every wand'ring bark,
Whose worth's unknown, although his height be taken.
Love's not Time's fool, though rosy lips and cheeks
Within his bending sickle's compass come;
Love alters not with his brief hours and weeks,
But bears it out even to the edge of doom.
    If this be error and upon me proved,
      I never writ, nor no man ever loved.

# Letters between Winston Churchill and his wife, Clementine

*November 28, 1915*

To Winston

. . . But when I think of you my Dearest Darling, I forget all disappointment, bitterness or ambition & long to have you safe & warm & alive in my arms. Since you have re-become a soldier I look upon civilians of high or low degree with pity & indulgence—The wives of men over military age may be lucky but I am sorry for them being married to feeble & incompetent old men.

I think you will get this letter on your birthday & it brings you all my love & many passionate kisses—My Darling Darling Winston—I find my morning breakfast lonely without you, so Sarah fills your place & does her best to look almost exactly like you. I'm keeping the flag flying till you return by getting up early & having breakfast down-stairs.

*December 1, 1915*

*To Clementine*
*I reopen my envelope to tell you I have recd your dear letter of the 28th.*
*I reciprocate intensely the feelings of love & devotion you show to me.*
*My greatest good fortune in a life of brilliant experience has been to*
*find you, & to lead my life with you. I don't feel far away from you*
*out here at all. I feel vy near in my heart; & also I feel that the nearer*
*I get to honour, the nearer I am to you.*

# She Walks in Beauty

### Lord Byron

She walks in beauty, like the night
    Of cloudless climes and starry skies;
And all that's best of dark and bright
    Meet in her aspect and her eyes:
Thus mellowed to that tender light
    Which heaven to gaudy day denies.

One shade the more, one ray the less,
    Had half impaired the nameless grace
Which waves in every raven tress,
    Or softly lightens o'er her face;
Where thoughts serenely sweet express
    How pure, how dear their dwelling place.

And on that cheek, and o'er that brow,
    So soft, so calm, yet eloquent,
The smiles that win, the tints that glow,
    But tell of days in goodness spent,
A mind at peace with all below,
    A heart whose love is innocent!

# *American merchant Lyman Hodge to his fiancée, Mary Granger*

*February 10th, 1867*

*. . . and now, love, you with the warm heart and loving eyes, whose picture I kissed last night and whose lips I so often kiss in my dreams, whose love enriches me so bountifully with all pleasant memories and sweet anticipations, whose encircling arms shield me from so much evil and harm, whose caresses are so dear and so longed for awake and in slumber, making my heart beat faster, my flesh tremble and my brain giddy with delight,—whose feet I kiss and whose knees I embrace as a devotee kisses and embraces those of his idol,—my darling whose home is in my arms and whose resting place my bosom, who first came to them as a frightened bird but now loves to linger there till long after the midnight chimes have uttered their warning,—my life, with your generous womanly soul, my heart's keeper and my true lover,—Good night: a good night and a fair one to thy sleeping eyes and wearied limbs, the precurser of many bright, beautiful mornings when my kisses shall waken thee and my love shall greet thee.*

# To the Virgins, To Make Much of Time

### Robert Herrick

Gather ye rosebuds while ye may,
Old Time is still a-flying:
And this same flower that smiles today
Tomorrow will be dying.

The glorious lamp of heaven, the sun,
The higher he's a-getting,
The sooner will his race be run,
And nearer he's to setting.

That age is best which is the first,
When youth and blood are warmer;
But being spent, the worse, and worst
Times still succeed the former.

Then be not coy, but use your time,
And while ye may, go marry:
For having lost but once your prime,
You may for ever tarry.

# Poet John Keats to Fanny Brawne

*May 1920, Tuesday Morn.*

*My dearest Girl,*

*I wrote a Letter for you yesterday expecting to have seen your mother. I shall be selfish enough to send it though I know it may give you a little pain, because I wish you to see how unhappy I am for love of you, and endeavour as much as I can to entice you to give up your whole heart to me whose whole existence hangs upon you. You could not step or move an eyelid but it would shoot to my heart—I am greedy of you—Do not think of any thing but me. Do not live as if I was not existing—Do not forget me—But have I any right to say you forget me? Perhaps you think of me all day. Have I any right to wish you to be unhappy for me? You would forgive me for wishing it, if you knew the extreme passion I have that you should love me—and for you to love me as I do you, you must think of no one but me, much less write that sentence. . . .*

J.K.

*No—my sweet Fanny—I am wrong. I do not want you to be unhappy—and yet I do, I must while there is so sweet a Beauty—my loveliest my darling! Good bye! I kiss you—O the torments!*

# When I Am with You

Rumi

When I am with you, we stay up all night.
When you are not here, I can't go to sleep.
Praise God for these two insomnias!
And the difference between them.

# From the Journal of Queen Victoria

*Already the 2nd day since our marriage; his love and gentleness is beyond everything, and to kiss that dear soft cheek, to press my lips to his, is heavenly bliss. I feel a purer more unearthly feel than I ever did. Oh! was ever woman so blessed as I am.*

# To My Dear and Loving Husband

### Anne Bradstreet

If ever two were one, then surely we.
If ever man were loved by wife, then thee;
If ever wife was happy in a man,
Compare with me ye women if you can.
I prize thy love more than whole mines of gold,
Or all the riches that the East doth hold.
My love is such that rivers cannot quench,
Nor ought but love from thee, give recompense.
Thy love is such I can no way repay,
The heavens reward thee manifold I pray.
Then while we live, in love let's so persevere,
That when we live no more, we may live ever.

# Love Song

## William Carlos Williams

Sweep the house clean,
hang fresh curtains
in the windows
put on a new dress
and come with me!
The elm is scattering
its little loaves
of sweet smells
from a white sky!
Who shall hear of us
in the time to come?
Let him say there was
a burst of fragrance
from black branches.

# Telegram from writer Anne Sexton to her husband, Alfred Muller

*September 27, 1963*

VENICE IMPOSSIBLY BEAUTIFUL
YOUR LETTERS

BETTER THAN WINE STAYING 8
DAYS PLEASE

WRITE HERE JUMPING CATFISH
LOVE

# My Mistress' Eyes Are Nothing Like the Sun

**William Shakespeare**

My mistress' eyes are nothing like the sun;
Coral is far more red than her lips' red:
If snow be white, why then her breasts are dun;
If hairs be wires, black wires grow on her head.
I have seen roses damaskt, red and white,
But no such roses see I in her cheeks;
And in some perfumes is there more delight
Than in the breath that from my mistress reeks.
I love to hear her speak, yet well I know
That music hath a far more pleasing sound;
I grant I never saw a goddess go;
My mistress, when she walks, treads on the ground.
    And yet, by heaven, I think my love as rare
    As any she belied with false compare.

# French intellectual Simone de Beauvoir to philosopher Jean-Paul Sartre

*February 16, 1940*

*I'm altogether immersed in the happiness I derive from seeing you. Nothing else counts. I have you—little all-precious one, little beloved one—as much today as the day before yesterday when I could see you, and I'll have you till the day I die. After that, nothing of all that may happen to me really has any importance. Not only am I not sad, I'm even deeply happy and secure. Even the tenderest memories—of all your dear expressions, or your little arms cradling the pillow in the morning—aren't painful to me. I feel myself all enfolded and sustained by your love.*

# How Do I Love Thee?

### Elizabeth Barrett Browning

How do I love thee? Let me count the ways.
I love thee to the depth and breadth and height
My soul can reach, when feeling out of sight
For the ends of Being and ideal Grace.
I love thee to the level of everyday's
Most quiet need, by sun and candle-light.
I love thee freely, as men strive for Right;
I love thee purely, as they turn from Praise.
I love thee with the passion put to use
In my old griefs, and with my childhood's faith.
I love thee with a love I seemed to lose
With my lost saints!—I love thee with the breath,
Smiles, tears, of all my life!—and, if God choose,
I shall but love thee better after death.

# A poem from E. B. White to his wife, Katharine

Natural History

*The spider, dropping down from twig,*
*Unwinds a thread of her devising:*
*A thin, premeditated rig*
*To use in rising.*

*And all the journey down through space,*
*In cool descent, and loyal-hearted,*
*She builds a ladder to the place*
*From which she started.*

*Thus I, gone forth, as spiders do,*
*In spider's web a truth discerning,*
*Attach one silken strand to you*
*For my returning.*

# Jenny Kiss'd Me

Leigh Hunt

Jenny kiss'd me when we met,
  Jumping from the chair she sat in;
Time, you thief, who love to get
  Sweets into your list, put that in!
Say I'm weary, say I'm sad,
  Say that health and wealth have miss'd me,
Say I'm growing old, but add,
  Jenny kiss'd me.

# A proposal from Simon Fallowfield, a farmer, to Mary Foster

*My Dear Miss,*

*I now take up my pen to write to you hoping these few lines will find you well as it leaves me at present Thank God for it. You will perhaps be surprised that I should make so bold as to write to you who is such a lady and I hope you will not be vex at me for it. I hardly dare say what I want, I am so timid about ladies, and my heart trimmels like a hespin. But I once seed in a book that faint heart never won fair lady, so here goes.*

*I am a farmer in a small way and my age is rather more than forty years and my mother lives with me and keeps my house, and she has been very poorly lately and cannot stir about much and I think I should be more comfortabler with a wife.*

*I have had my eye on you a long time and I think you are a very nice young woman and one that would make me happy if only you*

*think so. We keep a servant girl to milk three kye and do the work in
the house, and she goes out a bit in the summer to gadder wickens and
she snags a few of turnips in the back kend. I do a piece of work on the
farm myself and attends Pately Market, and I sometimes show a few
sheep and I feeds between 3 & 4 pigs agen Christmas, and the same is
very useful in the house to make pies and cakes and so forth, and I
sells the hams to help pay for the barley meal.*

*I have about 73 pund in Naisbro Bank and we have a nice little
parlour downstairs with a blue carpet, and an oven on the side of the
fireplace and the old woman on the other side smoking. The Golden
Rules claimed up on the walls above the long settle, and you could sit*

## SIMON FALLOWFIELD TO MARY FOSTER

*all day in the easy chair and knit and mend my kytles and leggums,
and you could make the tea ready agin I come in, and you could make
butter for Pately Market, and I would drive you to church every
Sunday in the spring cart, and I would do all that bees in my power to
make you happy. So I hope to hear from you. I am in desprit and
Yurnest, and will marry you at May Day, or if my mother dies afore I
shall want you afore. If only you will accept of me, my dear, we could
be very happy together.*

*I hope you will let me know your mind by return of post, and if
you are favourable I will come up to scratch. So no more at present
from your well-wisher and true love—*

*Simon Fallowfield*


*P.S. I hope you will say nothing about this. If you will not accept of me
I have another very nice woman in my eye, and I think I shall marry
her if you do not accept of me, but I thought you would suit me mother
better, she being very crusty at times. So I tell you now before you come,
she will be Maister.*


Foster rejected Fallowfield's proposal.

# somewhere i have never travelled gladly beyond

E. E. Cummings

somewhere i have never travelled, gladly beyond
any experience, your eyes have their silence:
in your most frail gesture are things which enclose me,
or which i cannot touch because they are too near

your slightest look easily will unclose me
though i have closed myself as fingers,
you open always petal by petal myself as Spring opens
(touching skillfully, mysteriously) her first rose

or if your wish be to close me, i and
my life will shut very beautifully, suddenly,
as when the heart of this flower imagines
the snow carefully everywhere descending;

nothing which we are to perceive in this world equals
the power of your intense fragility: whose texture
compels me with the colour of its countries,
rendering death and forever with each breathing

(i do not know what it is about you that closes
and opens; only something in me understands
the voice of your eyes is deeper than all roses)
nobody, not even the rain, has such small hands

# Tsarina Alexandra to her husband, Tsar Nicholas II of Russia

*December 30, 1915*

*Off you go again alone & it's with a very heavy heart I part from you. No more kisses and tender caresses for ever so long—I want to bury myself into you, hold you tight in my arms, make you feel the intense love of mine. You are my very life Sweetheart, and every separation gives such endless heartache. . . . Goodbye my Angel, Husband of my heart I envy my flowers that will accompany you. I press you tightly to my breast, kiss every sweet place with gentle tender love. . . God bless and protect you, guard you from all harm, guide you safely & firmly into the new year. May it bring glory & sure peace, & the reward for all this war has cost you. I gently press my lips to yours & try to forget everything, gazing into your lovely eyes—I lay on your precious breast, rested my tired head upon it still. This morning I tried to gain calm & strength for the separation. Goodbye wee one, Lovebird, Sunshine, Huzy mine, Own!*

# Nuptial Sleep

## Dante Gabriel Rossetti

At length their long kiss severed, with sweet smart:
    And as the last slow sudden drops are shed
    From sparkling eaves when all the storm has fled,
So singly flagged the pulses of each heart.
Their bosoms sundered, with the opening start
    Of married flowers to either side outspread
    From the knit stem; yet still their mouths, burnt red,
Fawned on each other where they lay apart.

Sleep sank them lower than the tide of dreams,
    And their dreams watched them sink, and slid away.
Slowly their souls swam up again, through gleams
    Of watered light and dull drowned waifs of day;
Till from some wonder of new woods and streams
    He woke, and wondered more: for there she lay.

# French actress Sarah Bernhardt to writer Jean Richepin

*1883*

*Carry me off into the blue skies of tender loves, roll me in dark clouds, tramp me with your thunderstorms, break me in your angry rages. But love me, my adored love.*

# The Author to His Wife, of a Woman's Eloquence

### Sir John Harrington

My Mall, I mark that when you mean to prove me
To buy a velvet gown, or some rich border,
Thou call'st me good sweet heart, thou swear'st to love me,
Thy locks, thy lips, thy looks, speak all in order,
Thou think'st, and right thou think'st, that these do move me,
That all these severally thy suit do further:
    But shall I tell thee what most thy suit advances?
    Thy fair smooth words? no, no, thy fair smooth haunches.

# Letters between English writer John Middleton Murry and his wife, Katherine Mansfield

14 January 1918

*To Katherine*

*. . . As I got up from my chair, I saw your letter lying on the little round table in front of me. I had to kiss it: then I stood by the fire and looked at the clock, and loved you so much that I thought my heart would burst. I wondered whether some thing would tell you that I was full of love of you, wanting you to know I loved you so deeply, at a quarter to twelve on Monday night. Then I got down your photograph. It's stuck in a corner of the looking glass. And I was knocked all of a heap by your beauty again. It's the photo where you have the black jacket on, and the marguerite on your button-hole. And there is all that wonderful, secret child-ness, trembling about that impossibly*

*delicate mouth. You darling, darling, darling. That's only the first words of what I said to you. You exquisite, incredible woman.*

*27 January 1918*

*To John*
*My love for you tonight is so deep and tender that it seems to be outside myself as well. I am fast shut up like a little lake in the embrace of some big mountains. If you were to climb up the mountains, you would see me down below, deep and shining—and quite fathomless, my dear. You might drop your heart into me and you'd never hear it touch bottom. I love you—I love you—Goodnight. Oh, Bogey, what it is to love like this!*

# Come, and Be My Baby

Maya Angelou

The highway is full of big cars going nowhere fast
And folks is smoking anything that'll burn
Some people wrap their lives around a cocktail glass
And you sit wondering
where you're going to turn
I got it.
Come. And be my baby.
Some prophets say the world is gonna end tomorrow
But others say we've got a week or two
The paper is full of every kind of blooming horror
And you sit wondering
What you're gonna do.
I got it.
Come. And be my baby.

Ellen
H. Clapsaddle

# British explorer Captain Robert F. Scott to his wife

*January 1st, 1911*

*At Christmas I got your letter. . .I could hear you saying the words
. . .I sent glad thoughts to you, I wonder if you felt them. I looked out-
of-doors in the evening on a truly Christmassy scene. On all sides an
expanse of snow covered floes, a dull grey sky shedding fleecy snow
flakes, every rope and spar had its little white deposit like the sugaring
on a cake. A group of penguins were having highly amusing antics
close by, and the sounds of revelry followed behind, but on the white
curtain of feathery crystals I tried to picture your face, and I said God
bless her for having been an unselfish wife, and the best of friends to an
undeserving man. . .*

# Although I Conquer All the Earth

**Anonymous**

Although I conquer all the earth,
Yet for me there is only one city.
In that city there is for me only one house;
And in that house, one room only;
And in that room, a bed.
And one woman sleeps there,
The shining joy and jewel of all my kingdom.

# American president Thomas Woodrow Wilson to his wife, Ellen

May 9, 1886

*. . . I've been reckoning up, in a tumultuous, heartful sort of way, the value of my little wife to me. I can't state the result—there are no terms of value in which it can be stated—but perhaps I can give you some idea of what its proportions would be if it were stated. She has taken all real pain out of my life: her wonderful loving sympathy exalts even my occasional moods of despondency into a sort of hallowed sadness out of which I come stronger and better. She has given to my ambitions a meaning, an assurance, and a purity which they never had before: with her by my side, ardently devoted to me and to my cause, understanding all my thoughts and all my aims, I feel that I can make the utmost of every power I possess. She has brought into my life the sunshine which was needed to keep it from growing stale and morbid: that has steadily been bringing back into my spirits their old gladness and boyhood, their old delight in play and laughter: —that sweetest sunshine of deep,*

*womanly love, unfailing, gentle patience, even happy spirits, and*
*spontaneous mirth, that is purest, swiftest tonic to a spirit prone to fret*
*and apt to flag. She has given me that perfect rest of heart and mind of*
*whose existence I had never so much as dreamed before she came to me,*
*which springs out of assured oneness of hope and sympathy—and*
*which, for me, means life and success. Above all she has given me*
*herself to live for! Her arms are able to hold me up against the world:*
*her eyes are able to charm away every care; her words are my solace and*
*inspiration and all because her love is my life. . .*

# Answer to a Child's Question

Samuel Taylor Coleridge

Do you ask what the birds say? The Sparrow, the Dove,
The Linnet and Thrush say, "I love and I love!"
In the winter they're silent—the wind is so strong;
What it says, I don't know, but it sings a loud song.
But green leaves, and blossoms, and sunny warm weather;
And singing, and loving—all come back together.
But the Lark is so brimful of gladness and love,
The green fields below him, the blue sky above,
That he sings, and he sings; and for ever sings he—
"I love my Love, and my Love loves me!"

# *Notes between actress Rachel Felix and Prince Joinville*

*1840*

To Rachel
*Where?*
*When?*
*How Much?*

To the Prince
*Your place.*
*Tonight.*
*Free.*

# Such Different Wants

Robert Bly

The board floats on the river.
The board wants nothing
but is pulled from beneath
on into deeper waters.

And the elephant dwelling
on the mountain wants
a trumpet so its dying cry
can be heard by the stars.

The wakeful heron striding
through reeds at dawn wants
the god of sun and moon
to see his long skinny neck.

You must say what you want.
I want to be the man
and I am who will love you
when your hair is white.

# Writer Nathaniel Hawthorne to his fiancée, Sophia Peabody

*Boston, September 23d, 1839, ¹/₂ past 6 P.M.*

*Belovedest little wife – sweetest Sophie Hawthorne – what a delicious walk that was, last Thursday! It seems to me, now, as if I could really remember every footstep of it. It is almost as distinct as the recollection of those walks, in which my earthly form did really tread beside your own, and my arm uphold you; and, indeed, it has the same character as those heavenly ramblings;—for did we tread on earth even then? Oh no—our souls went far away among the sunset clouds, and wherever there was ethereal beauty, there were we, our true selves; and it was there that we grew into each other, and became a married pair. Dearest, I love to date our marriage as far back as possible; and I feel sure that the tie had been formed, and our union had become indissoluble, even before we sat down together on the steps of the 'house of spirits'. How beautiful and blessed those hours appear to*

*me! True; we are far more
conscious of our relation, and
therefore infinitely happier, now,
than we were then; but still those
remembrances are among the most
precious treasures of my soul. It is
not past happiness; it makes a
portion of our present bliss. And
thus, doubtless, even amid the
Joys of Heaven, we shall love to
look back to our earthly bliss, and
treasure it forever in the sum of
our infinitely accumulating
happiness. Perhaps not a single
pressure of the hand, not a
glance, not a sweet and tender tone, not one kiss, but will be repeated
sometime or other in our memory.*

*Sept 25th, Morning.*

*Dove, I have but a single moment to embrace you. Tell Sophie
Hawthorne I love her. Has she a partiality to your own, own,*

*Husband.*

# When You Are Old

### William Butler Yeats

When you are old and grey and full of sleep,
And nodding by the fire, take down this book,
And slowly read, and dream of the soft look
Your eyes had once, and of their shadows deep;

How many loved your moments of glad grace,
And loved your beauty with love false or true,
But one man loved the pilgrim soul in you,
And loved the sorrows of your changing face;

And bending down beside the glowing bars,
Murmur, a little sadly, how Love fled
And paced upon the mountains overhead
And hid his face amid a crowd of stars.

# Letters between English poets Robert Browning and Elizabeth Barrett Browning

*To Elizabeth*

*I love your verses with all my heart, dear Miss Barrett,—and this is no off-hand complimentary letter that I shall write,—whatever else, no prompt matter-of-course recognition of your genius and there a graceful and natural end of the thing: since the day last week when I first read your poems, I quite laugh to remember how I have been turning and turning again in my mind what I should be able to tell you of their effect upon me—for in the first flush of delight I thought I would this once get out of my habit of purely passive enjoyment, when I do really enjoy, and thoroughly justify my admiration—perhaps even, as a loyal fellow-craftsman should, try and find fault and do you some little*

*good to be proud of hereafter! —but nothing comes of it all—so into me
has it gone, and part of me has it become, this great living poetry of
yours, not a flower of which but took root and grew . . . oh, how
different that is from lying to be dried and pressed flat and prized
highly and put in a book with a proper account at top and bottom,
and shut up and put away . . . and the book called a "Flora," besides!
After all, I need not give up the thought of doing that, too, in time;
because even now, talking with whoever is worthy, I can give a reason
for my faith in one and another excellence, the fresh strange music, the
affluent language, the exquisite pathos and true new brave thought—
but in this addressing myself to you, your own self, and for the first
time, my feeling rises altogether. I do, as I say, love these Books with all
my heart—and I love you too: do you know I was once not very far
from seeing—really seeing you? Mr. Kenyorh said to me one morning
"would you like to see Miss Barrett?"—then he went to announce
me,—then he returned . . . you were too unwell—and now it is years
ago—and I feel as at some untoward passage in my travels—as if I
had been close, so close, to some world's-wonder in chapel or crypt, . . .
only a screen to push and I might have entered— but there was some
slight . . . so it now seems . . . slight and just-sufficient bar to*

*admission, and the half-opened door shut, and I went home my*
*thousands of miles, and the sight was never to be! Well, these Poems*
*were to be—and this true thankful joy and pride with which I feel*
*myself.*

*January 10, 1846*

*To Robert*
*It seems to me, to myself, that no man was ever before to any woman*
*what you are to me—the fulness must be in proportion, you know, to the*
*vacancy . . . and only I know what was behind—the long wilderness*
*without the blossoming rose . . . and the capacity for happiness, like a*
*black gaping hole, before this silver flooding. Is it wonderful that I*
*should stand as in a dream, and disbelieve—not you—but my own*
*fate? Was ever any one taken suddenly from a lampless dungeon and*
*placed upon the pinnacle of a mountain, without the head turning*
*round and the heart turning faint, as mine do?*

# Love's Philosophy

Percy Bysshe Shelley

The fountains mingle with the river
   And the rivers with the Ocean,
The winds of Heaven mix for ever
   With a sweet emotion;
Nothing in the world is single;
   All things by a law divine
In one spirit meet and mingle,
   Why not I with thine?—

See the mountains kiss high Heaven
   And the waves clasp one another;
No sister-flower would be forgiven
   If it disdained its brother;
And the sunlight clasps the earth
   And the moonbeams kiss the sea:
What is all this sweet work worth
   If thou kiss not me?

# Letters between American president John Adams and his wife, Abigail

*To Abigail*

*Next month completes three years that I have been devoted to the service of liberty. A slavery it has been to me, whatever the world may think of it. To a man whose attachments to his family are as strong as mine, absence alone from such a wife and such children would be a great sacrifice. But in addition to this separation what have I not done? What have I not suffered? What have I not hazarded? These are questions that I may ask you, but I will ask such questions of none else. Let the cymbals of popularity tinkle still. Let the butterflies of fame glitter with their wings. I shall envy neither their music nor their colors. The loss of property affects me little. All other hard things I despise, but the loss of your company and that of my dear babes for so long a time, I consider as a loss of so much solid happiness. The*

*tender social feelings of my heart which have distressed me beyond all
utterance in my most busy active scenes as well as in the numerous
hours of melancholy solitude, are known only to God and my own soul.*

*To John
My Dearest Friend,
. . . should I draw you the picture of my heart it would be what I hope
you would still love though it contained nothing new. The early*

*possession you obtained there, and the
absolute power you have obtained over it,
leaves not the smallest space unoccupied.
I look back to the early days of our
acquaintance and friendship as to the
days of love and innocence, and, with an
indescribable pleasure, I have seen near a
score of years roll over our heads with an
affection heightened and improved by
time, nor have the dreary years of absence
in the smallest degree effaced from my
mind the image of the dear untitled man
to whom I gave my heart.*

# Shall I Compare Thee to a Summer's Day?

### William Shakespeare

Shall I compare thee to a summer's day?
Thou art more lovely and more temperate:
Rough winds do shake the darling buds of May,
And summer's lease hath all too short a date:
Sometime too hot the eye of heaven shines,
And often is his gold complexion dimm'd;
And every fair from fair sometime declines,
By chance or nature's changing course untrimm'd;
But thy eternal summer shall not fade,
Nor lose possession of that fair thou owest;
Nor shall Death brag thou wander'st in his shade,
When in eternal lines to time thou grow'st:
    So long as men can breathe, or eyes can see,
    So long lives this, and this gives life to thee.

# English poet Rupert Brooke to his sweetheart, Noël Oliver

*October 2nd, 1911*

*I have a thousand images of you in an hour; all different and all coming back to the same . . .*

*And we love. And we've got the most amazing secrets and understandings. Noël, whom I love, who is so beautiful and wonderful. I think of you eating omelette on the ground. I think of you once against a sky line: and on the hill that Sunday morning. And that night was wonderfullest of all. The light and shadow & quietness & the rain & the wood. And you. You are so beautiful and wonderful that I daren't write to you . . . And kinder than God. Your arms and lips and hair and shoulders and voice—you*

# Variation

Federico García Lorca

That still pool of the air
under the branch of an echo.

That still pool of the water
under a frond of bright stars.

That still pool of your mouth
under a thicket of kisses.

# English poet Thomas Otway to Mrs. Barry, an actress

Between 1678 and 1688

*Could I see you without passion, or be absent from you without pain, I need not beg your pardon for thus renewing my vows that I love you more than health, or any happiness here or hereafter. Everything you do is a new charm to me, and though I have languished for seven long tedious years of desire, jealously despairing, yet every minute I see you I still discover something new and more bewitching. Consider how I love you; what would I not renounce or enterprise for you? I must have you mine, or I am miserable, and nothing but knowing which shall be the happy hour can make the rest of my years that are to come tolerable. Give me a word or two of comfort, or resolve never to look on me more, for I cannot bear a kind look and after it a cruel denial. This minute my heart aches for you; and, if I cannot have a right in yours, I wish it would ache till I could complain to you no longer.*

# The Passionate Shepherd to His Love

### Christopher Marlowe

Come live with me and be my love,
And we will all the pleasures prove
That valleys, groves, hills, and fields,
Woods, or steepy mountain yields.

And we will sit upon the rocks,
Seeing the shepherds feed their flocks,
By shallow rivers to whose falls
Melodious birds sing madrigals.

And I will make thee beds of roses
And a thousand fragrant posies,
A cap of flowers, and a kirtle
Embroidered all with leaves of myrtle;

A gown made of the finest wool
Which from our pretty lambs we pull;
Fair lined slippers for the cold,
With buckles of the purest gold;

A belt of straw and ivy buds,
With coral clasps and amber studs:
And if these pleasures may thee move,
Come live with me, and be my love.

The shepherds' swains shall dance and sing
For thy delight each May morning:
If these delights thy mind may move,
Then live with me and be my love.

# Napoleon Bonaparte to his wife, Josephine

*I love you no longer; on the contrary, I detest you. You are a wretch, truly perverse, truly stupid, a real Cinderella. You never write to me at all, you do not love your husband; you know the pleasure that your letters give him yet you cannot even manage to write him half a dozen lines, dashed off in a moment! What then do you do all day, Madame? What business is so vital that it robs you of the time to write to your faithful lover? What attachment can be stifling and pushing aside the love, the tender and constant love, which you promised him? Who can this wonderful lover be who takes up your every moment, rules your days, and prevents you from devoting your attention to your husband? Beware, Josephine; one fine night the doors will be broken down and there I shall be.*